OCT   2012

discover countries

Discover Afghanistan

Richard Spilsbury

PowerKiDS press.

New York

Published in 2012 by the Rosen Publishing Group, Inc.
29 East 21st Street, New York, NY 10010

First Edition

Concept Design: Jason Billin
Editors: Nicola Edwards and Jennifer Sanderson
Designer: Amy Sparks
Picture Research: Amy Sparks
Consultant: Elaine Jackson

Photographs:
Cover, (left) Shutterstock/Lizette Potgieter, (right) Shutterstock/Lebedev Alexey; 1, Shutterstock/Lizette Potgieter; 3 (bottom), Shutterstock/Dana Ward, (top), Shutterstock/Tracing Tea; 4 (map), Stefan Chabluk; 5, Corbis/Robert Harding World Imagery; 6, Dreamstime/Lapstraked; 7, Shutterstock/Lebedev Alexey; 8–9, Shutterstock/Tracing Tea; 10, iStockphoto/Mie Ahmt; 11, Shutterstock/Lebedev Alexey; 12, Shutterstock/Dana Ward; 13, Corbis/Caroline Penn; 14, Corbis/STR/epa; 15, Shutterstock/Lizette Potgieter; 16, Dreamstime/Sagear; 17, Shutterstock/Lizette Potgieter; 18, Corbis/Omar Sobhani/Reuters; 19, Shutterstock/Dana Ward; 20, Corbis/HOSSEIN FATEMI/epa; 21, Shutterstock/Lizette Potgieter; 22, iStockphoto/Jean Nordmann; 23, Shutterstock/Lizette Potgieter; 24, Photos-to-go; 25 (top), Corbis/David Trilling, (bottom), Shutterstock/Lizette Potgieter; 26, Shutterstock/Dana Ward; 27, Shutterstock/Nikm; 28, Shutterstock/Nikm; 29, Shutterstock/Dennis Donohue.

Library of Congress Cataloging-in-Publication Data

Spilsbury, Richard, 1963–
 Discover Afghanistan / by Richard Spilsbury. — 1st ed.
     p. cm. — (Discover countries)
 Includes index.
 ISBN 978-1-4488-6619-9 (library binding) — ISBN 978-1-4488-7044-8 (pbk.) —
 ISBN 978-1-4488-7045-5 (6-pack)
 1. Afghanistan—Juvenile literature. I. Title.
 DS351.5.S65 2012
 958.1—dc23

                              2011029059

Manufactured in Malaysia

CPSIA Compliance Information: Batch #WW2102PK: For Further Information contact Rosen Publishing, New York, New York at 1-800-237-9932

Contents

Discovering Afghanistan

Afghanistan is a mountainous country in central Asia that is a little bit smaller than Texas. It is a poor country, damaged by years of fighting, and is struggling to improve its economy.

A New Regime

After years of political turmoil following invasion by the Soviet Union in 1979, the Taliban party took control of Afghanistan in 1996. The Taliban was popular among many people because it promised peace. However, it brought in some harsh rules. The Taliban

Afghanistan Statistics

Area: 251,827 sq. miles (652,230 sq. km)

Capital City: Kabul

Government Type: Islamic Republic

Bordering Countries: China, Iran, Pakistan, Tajikistan, Turkmenistan, Uzbekistan

Currency: Afghani (AFA)

Language: Afghan Persian or Dari (official) 50%, Pashto (official) 35%, Turkic languages (primarily Uzbek and Turkmen) 11%, 30 minor languages (primarily Balochi and Pashai) 4%

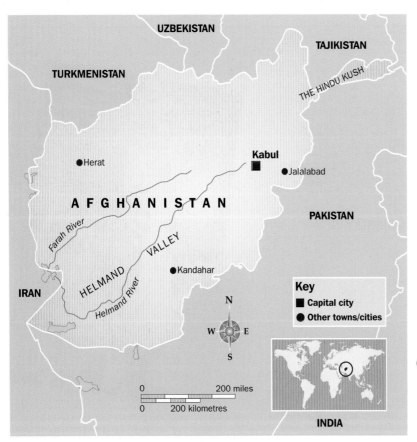

Afghanistan is a landlocked country. It borders Pakistan to the east and Iran to the west. The countries to the north of Afghanistan were once part of the Soviet Union.

punished people by public whipping and execution. Girls were not allowed to go to school and women could not work. It also welcomed terrorist groups, such as Osama bin Laden's Al Qaeda, into the country.

Election

After the Al Qaeda attacks on September 11, 2001, forces from the USA and other countries invaded Afghanistan. They toppled the Taliban and helped anti-Taliban forces take power. In 2004, Hamid Karzai became Afghanistan's first democratically elected president. In recent years, life has improved for many people in Afghanistan. For example, all children have a better chance of a good education. However, since 2008 Taliban forces have re-emerged in Afghanistan.

Future Challenges

Afghanistan's weak economy is partly a result of its troubled recent history. The country has also been unable to invest in and profit from its oil, gas, and other natural resources. This means that its people rely on foreign help, such as food aid. In the future, Afghans hope that a stable government will bring peace and security to their country. This will help the economy recover and the country's dramatic scenery and rich history might attract visitors and more investment.

⬤ Although Kabul bears the scars of the country's past turmoil, reconstruction is making it a busy capital city.

DID YOU KNOW?

Hundreds of tanks lie rusting near Kabul. They were abandoned when the Soviet Union, which had occupied Afghanistan since 1979, left in 1989.

Landscape and Climate

Afghanistan is a landlocked country with no coastline. In spring, its many rivers are filled by melted snow from the mountains. However, there is limited freshwater available in summer because there are few lakes and most rivers dry up.

High and Low

A spine of high mountains stretches from the northeast to the southwest of Afghanistan. These mountains include the Hindu Kush, which borders Northern Pakistan and Tajikistan, the high Pamirs, bordering China, and smaller mountains in the country's center (see map on page 4). There are flatter regions near the borders with Iran in the southwest and Turkmenistan and Uzbekistan in the north. The mountains are one of the reasons that the Afghan government is weak. This is because Afghans living in mountainous areas are isolated from Kabul and often ruled by local tribal leaders.

Facts at a Glance

Land Area: 251,827 sq. miles (652,230 sq. km)

Highest Point: Noshak 24,557 feet (7,485 m)

Lowest Point: Amu Darya 846 feet (258 m)

Longest River: Helmand River 715 miles (1,150 km) long

Although the thick snow on mountains in Afghanistan is beautiful, it blocks roads and causes avalanches that threaten settlements.

▶ In spring and summer, snowmelt fills the rivers in Afghanistan's mountain valleys.

Climate

Afghanistan has a continental climate. This means that it has warm, dry summers and very cold, snowy winters. The country gets most of its rain in spring. The mountains prevent the summer monsoon winds that blow from the Indian Ocean from reaching Afghanistan. In summer, the flatter regions of the southwest become very hot, dry, and dusty.

Extreme Weather

The country also suffers some extreme weather events. In summer, the hot, dry "wind of 120 days" brings intense heat and drought and can cause sandstorms in the south and the west. It carries dust and can reach speeds of up to 110 miles per hour (180 km/h). This wind makes farming difficult and causes life-threatening health conditions in people, such as heat stroke. In the mountains, there are frequent blizzards in winter.

DID YOU KNOW?
The first windmills were invented in Afghanistan, Iran, and Iraq. These used the winds that blow from the mountains over the plains to grind grain.

Temperature °F (°C)

Kabul: Average Temperature

77 (25)
68 (20)
59 (15)
50 (10)
41 (5)
32 (0)
23 (-5)

Jan Feb Mar Apr May Jun Jul Aug Sep Oct Nov Dec
Months

Rainfall in. (mm)

Kabul: Average Rainfall

4.7 (120)
4 (100)
3.1 (80)
2.4 (60)
1.6 (40)
0.8 (20)
0 (0)

Jan Feb Mar Apr May Jun Jul Aug Sep Oct Nov Dec
Months

Population and Health

Afghanistan has a growing population that is made up of a variety of tribal peoples. Almost all Afghans face health challenges.

Changing Population

The majority of people in Afghanistan are quite young because families tend to have many children. According to the UN, the population was 28 million in 2009 and could grow to more than 110 million by 2050. The population has gone up and down in the past because of violence and war. In the 1980s and 1990s, hundreds of thousands of people left to escape the fighting, but many have since returned.

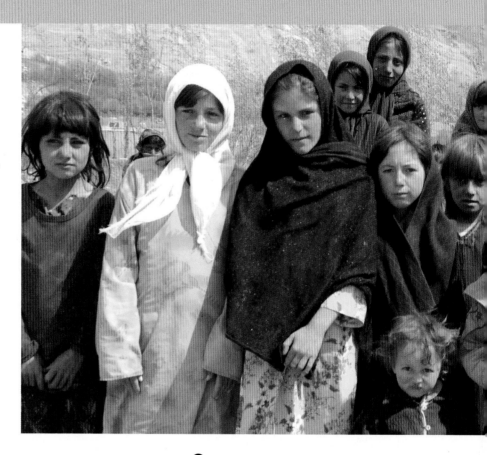

⬤ Young people make up the majority of many Afghan communities. Nearly half the population is 14 years old or younger.

Tribal Groups

There are many tribal groups in Afghanistan. The Pashtuns are the largest group and are found in the south and the east. Traditionally, Pashtuns were farmers. They speak Pashto. The Tajik people in the northeast were traditionally traders. They speak Dari. The main groups in north-central Afghanistan are the Hazaras, Tajiks, and Uzbeks. Across the country, more than 30 different languages are spoken and many people are bilingual.

Facts at a Glance

Total Population: 28.2 million

Life Expectancy at Birth: 45 years

Children Dying Before the Age of Five: 25.7%

Ethnic Composition: Pashtun 42%, Tajik 27%, Hazara 9%, Uzbek 9%, Aimak 4%, Turkmen 3%, Baloch 2%, other 4%

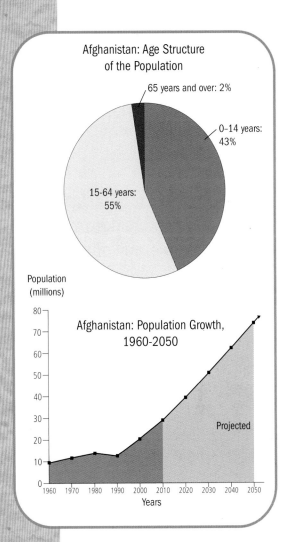

Afghanistan: Age Structure of the Population

65 years and over: 2%
0-14 years: 43%
15-64 years: 55%

Population (millions)

Afghanistan: Population Growth, 1960-2050

Projected

Years

Health, Dangers, and Disease

There are few doctors and hospitals in Afghanistan. One-sixth of Afghans have no access to any healthcare. The country has some of the world's highest infant, child, and maternal mortality rates. About 70 percent of Afghans have no access to clean water, so the risk of catching infectious diseases, such as diarrhea and typhoid, from dirty water is high. Another danger is from land mines left by Soviet and other foreign troops. There are 30 times more amputations each year in Afghanistan than there are in the USA because people accidentally step on or pick up the abandoned land mines.

DID YOU KNOW?
Many Afghans now speak some English and new words have been invented. For example, "gadwad" is Pashto for messy and the new word "gadwadation" means a messy situation.

Settlements and Living

During the years of war since the 1980s, about half a million homes were destroyed, along with many power plants, hospitals, and other buildings. With foreign help, the Afghans are rebuilding their settlements.

Rural and Urban

More people are moving to Afghanistan's cities every year. This is partly because foreign organizations have paid to rebuild streets ruined by war and this has created many jobs. Some farmers have moved to the cities because of failing crops, for example after a drought in 2000. People are also leaving some rural areas because of fighting with the Taliban.

Facts at a Glance

Urban Population: 22.4% (6.3 million)

Rural Population: 77.6% (21.9 million)

Population of Largest City: 3.3 million (Kabul)

⊽ Houses in this traditional mountain village are clustered together for shelter. Despite the dry landscape, the trees are a sign that a river flows through the valley.

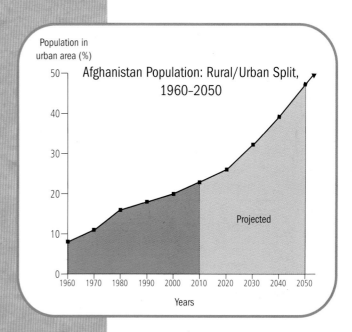

◀ Slum settlements of rapidly built homes are spreading to cover slopes on the outskirts of Kabul.

Poor Housing

Around one-third of Afghans live in inadequate or low-grade housing. This is partly because there is a shortage of building materials. It is also because, when more people move to the cities, the demand for land increases and landowners raise their prices. There are slums surrounding Kabul where the population has increased six times since 2001. Many new homes are badly built and have no water and electricity. Some, such as those on the hills surrounding Kabul, are at risk from floods and avalanches.

Settlements

In the countryside, most of the villages are built on the plains or in valleys. The villages are usually near rivers so that people have a supply of freshwater. In villages, many families live in small, rectangular, mud-brick houses.
The biggest cities are Kabul, Kandahar, Mazar-e-Sharif, and Herat. Afghanistan's cities are home to around 20 percent of the population, with 11 percent in Kabul alone. In cities, many people live in cramped apartment buildings.

DID YOU KNOW? Organizations such as the Federation of American Scientists are developing polystyrene houses for Afghans. These are light, easy to construct, and can survive the shaking caused by the earthquakes that happen there each year.

Population in urban area (%)

Afghanistan Population: Rural/Urban Split, 1960–2050

Projected

Years

Family Life

There may be many different tribes and languages spoken in Afghanistan, but family life is much the same across the country. Families are close-knit and spend most of their time together.

The Afghan Family

Many Afghans live in extended family groups. The head of the family is the oldest man, or patriarch. With him live his wife, their unmarried daughters, their sons, and their sons' wives and children. Younger members of the family are expected to show respect to older members and to always do as they are told. The family lives together in one home or in buildings in a shared compound. In city households, many families also have cousins or other relatives from the countryside staying with them. Under Taliban rule, only men went out to work and women looked after the family and the home, but this is changing as more women are employed.

▶ Afghan men typically live in the same homes as their children and grandchildren and have a great influence over their lives.

Facts at a Glance

Average Children per Childbearing Woman:
5.5 children

Average Household Size:
8 people

Getting Married

Patriarchs often choose partners for their children. This may be arranged a long time before the wedding, when they are still children. Sometimes, the bride and groom do not meet until the wedding day. Weddings last for days and include music, feasts, and different ceremonies. For example, the day before a wedding, the groom gives henna to his bride. She then has a "henna party," where her female relatives make intricate henna patterns on her hands.

Children

Once they are married, most wives move in with their husbands' families. Couples usually have several children. The older children are expected to look after younger children in the family. In the past, many Afghan men had up to four wives, but this is less common now. Divorce is rare. When a father dies, his sons usually share any inheritance. Daughters and widows seldom inherit any money or property. They have to depend on their brothers' or sons' generosity.

DID YOU KNOW?
Families have special feasts when boys reach the age of seven. At this age, boys are usually circumcised and they are allowed to wear a turban, like the adult men, for the first time.

Religion and Beliefs

Afghanistan's full name is "The Islamic Republic of Afghanistan." Religion and belief in Islam shape almost every aspect of people's lives there.

Islam in Afghanistan

Around 1,500 years ago, many people in Afghanistan followed the Buddhist religion. This changed when the Islamic Empire spread into the region in the seventh century. Today, 99 percent of people in Afghanistan are Muslim. Most are Sunni Muslims, but the Hazara people are Shiite Muslims. Sunni and Shiite Muslims follow different leaders and worship at different shrines or mosques. Sunni Taliban leaders persecuted Shiites when they were in power. Today, the government tries to prevent clashes by making sure there are some Shiite Muslims in the government.

DID YOU KNOW?

In 2001, members of the Taliban blew up two huge statues of Buddha in the mountainside at Bamiyan. The Taliban destroyed these ancient, world-famous statues because they were not Islamic.

⬇ Female followers of Islam in Afghanistan often wear body-covering garments, such as a burka, when outside their home—for example while visiting markets.

The Mullah

Mullahs are male Islamic religious leaders. They deliver Friday sermons and prayers in mosques, carry out marriages and funerals, and teach Islamic laws and beliefs. They are trusted community leaders in Afghanistan who help to sort out disputes and give advice on health matters, such as contraception. In 2009, the Afghan government trained mullahs to make more Afghan men aware of women's rights.

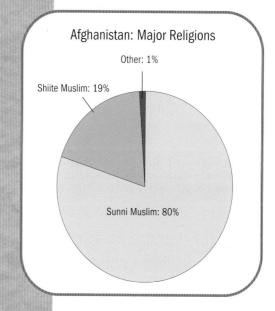

Afghanistan: Major Religions

- Other: 1%
- Shiite Muslim: 19%
- Sunni Muslim: 80%

Festivals

Two of the most important Islamic festivals in Afghanistan are Eid-el-Fitr and Eid-ul-Adha. Eid-el-Fitr marks the end of Ramadan. During Ramadan, Muslims do not eat or drink between sunrise and sunset. They do this to honor the time when the Koran was revealed to the prophet Muhammad. During Eid-el-Fitr there are services in mosques and families eat a special meal. Eid-ul-Adha remembers that the prophet Abraham was willing to sacrifice his son when God ordered him to. Muslims sacrifice a lamb as a symbol of what Abraham was prepared to do.

The Afghan New Year is in March and is known as Nowruz. Afghans usually celebrate with family picnics and by eating desserts, such as *haft-mehwah*. This contains fruit and nuts that symbolize the arrival of spring.

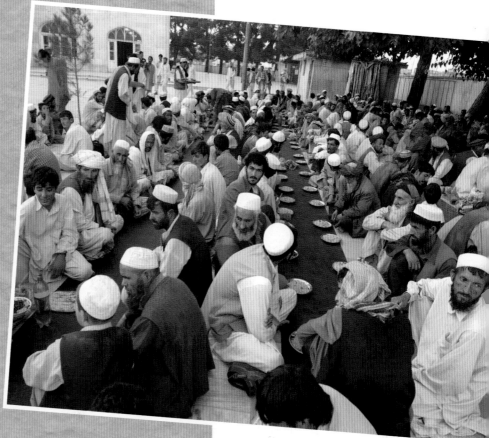

▼ Afghan men in Kabul have a meal of beans and rice to break their religious fast at dusk during Ramadan.

Education and Learning

The years of Soviet occupation, Taliban rule, and war with Allied forces have hurt education in Afghanistan. Schools were bombed and many teachers fled the country. Today, schools are being rebuilt and more children have the chance to learn.

Schools in Afghanistan

In 1996, there were only 650 public schools in the country. Religious schools, called madrassas, were the main centers of learning. After 2001, foreign aid was used to rebuild the education system. By 2008, six million children were enrolled at more than 9,000 schools. However, many children still miss out. Some schools do not have enough trained teachers. Some children live in the mountains, too far from a school. The Taliban also continues to threaten teachers and bomb schools, especially girls' schools.

Facts at a Glance

Children in Primary School:
Male 74%, Female 46%

Children in Secondary School:
Not known

Literacy Rate (Over 15 Years):
28%

⊙ These girls are taking part in the opening ceremony of a new girls' school in 2009. In good weather, some lessons take place outside, but the new building means school can continue when it is raining or snowing.

Adult Education

Recently, there has been an increase in adult education programs. For example, theater groups travel to remote villages to teach people things such as healthcare and how to get financial help from the government. Many of these courses are aimed at women. This is important because if women are educated, they can teach their daughters. Out of the eight universities in Afghanistan, the biggest is Kabul University, with around 20,000 students. In 2009, a quarter of the students at Afghan universities were women.

Literacy

Fewer than one-third of Afghans can read and write. One reason for this is that there are not many schools. The other problem is that most girls spend only four years at school. Some girls are expected to help cook, clean, and look after younger brothers and sisters. Some Muslims do not send their daughters to school because they do not think that girls, especially older girls, should mix with boys. Due to this lack of education, only 12 percent of the women in Afghanistan can read and write.

▶ Children in Afghanistan still study the Koran in mosques or madrassas. Boys and girls usually study separately.

Employment and Economy

In Afghanistan, 70 percent of the people live on less than $2 a day. However, the economy is slowly improving as money from foreign governments and charities is helping to pay for rebuilding. This is creating more jobs, although one-third of Afghans are still unemployed.

Jobs

One of the main causes of the high unemployment in Afghanistan is the damage done to industries by the years of war and Taliban rule. Another is that many adults are uneducated and cannot apply for some types of jobs.

Some industries in Afghanistan are improving, though. For example, there are more shops, hotels, and restaurants today. These cater to Afghans and foreign visitors working in construction, in security, or for charities. Gradually more and more women are working, too. Now there are female teachers, lawyers, and politicians. This is a stark contrast to the Taliban years when women were banned from working. However, women still make up less than 30 percent of the workforce.

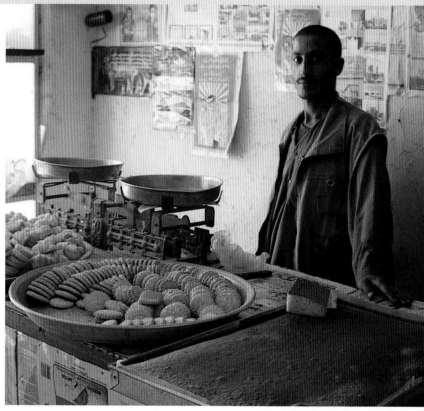

⬭ Bakeries like this one in Kabul are part of Afghanistan's growing service industry.

Facts at a Glance

Contributions to GDP:
  Agriculture: 31%
  Industry: 26%
  Services: 43%
Labor Force:
  Agriculture: 78.6%
  Industry: 5.7%
  Services: 15.7%
Female Labor Force:
  27% of total
Unemployment Rate: 35%

Black Market

The buying and selling of illegal goods is known as the black market. Black market trade makes up over half of Afghanistan's gross domestic product (GDP). The biggest earner is the production and sale of opium, a drug made from poppy flowers.

The opium trade is worth over $4 billion each year. Most of the heroin that is used by drug-takers in Europe comes from Afghan opium. Nearly a quarter of a million Afghans also use the drug. Many countries want Afghanistan to stop producing opium to help solve the world's drug problem. However, growing poppies is still the easiest way for many farmers to make money.

These British soldiers are patrolling a poppy field in Helmand province. This important opium-producing area is fiercely defended by Taliban fighters.

Industry and Trade

In the past, Afghanistan was occupied, or ruled, by many other countries, including Greece, the Soviet Union, and Great Britain. The countries wanted control of this region because of its position on trading routes between the East and West. Today, trucks carry goods on routes through Afghanistan to neighboring countries.

Natural Resources

Afghanistan has several valuable natural resources. Fossil fuels, including oil and gas, metals, such as copper, iron, and gold, and emeralds and other gemstones are all found there. In the past, mining and changing these resources into goods for export were important industries. Afghanistan used to export oil to the Soviet Union and made fertilizers from gas and coal.

◀ Although coal is mined, Afghanistan has other natural resources that are not exploited due to a lack of investment in mines.

However, during the long periods of war, the oil and gas wells were blocked up to prevent damage and these industries virtually died out. There are plans to reopen these wells after the fighting has stopped. Today, foreign businesses are investing in some mines. For example, Chinese companies are paying to open up copper and iron mines.

Industries

Most industries in Afghanistan use resources grown on its farms to produce goods. Some goods, such as leather shoes and soap, are sold within the country. Exported goods include sugar, salt, cotton textiles, and carpets. Carpets are the country's most valuable legal export. In 2007, approximately one million Afghans worked in the carpet industry. Many more had jobs keeping sheep to provide wool for the carpet makers.

Industries and factories sometimes face problems with power supply. Most of Afghanistan's electricity is supplied by neighboring countries, such as Tajikistan. The supply is limited and there are often blackouts when no electricity gets through to homes and businesses.

⚈ Carpet-weaving is often carried out on a small scale by Afghan women. Carpets are also made in large factories.

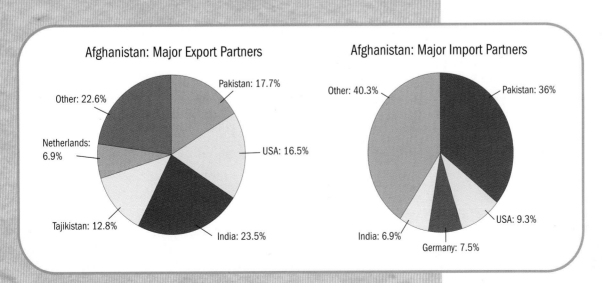

Afghanistan: Major Export Partners

- Pakistan: 17.7%
- Other: 22.6%
- USA: 16.5%
- Netherlands: 6.9%
- Tajikistan: 12.8%
- India: 23.5%

Afghanistan: Major Import Partners

- Other: 40.3%
- Pakistan: 36%
- USA: 9.3%
- Germany: 7.5%
- India: 6.9%

Farming and Food

Much of Afghanistan's farmland was damaged during the wars in its recent past. Some land has land mines on it and some was polluted when oil pipes were damaged. Farmland has also been damaged by overgrazing. In some areas, there is not enough rainfall or irrigation to grow food.

Crops and Livestock

Most farmers are subsistence farmers. They grow just enough food for their families and sell any that is left over. Afghan farmers grow wheat, barley, and rice.

▼ Afghan farmers plant rice shoots in flooded fields. The country produces around 70 percent of the rice it needs and imports the rest from Pakistan and Iran.

They farm fruits, such as apricots, dates, and grapes, nuts, including pistachios, and spices, such as saffron. The main growing areas are in the south where the land is more fertile. Livestock farmers raise cattle, goats, and fat-tailed sheep.

Helping Farmers

Many poor farmers grow poppies rather than food crops (see page 19). Taliban and tribal leaders often give farmers money in advance for this valuable crop. Today, the government encourages these farmers to grow food crops instead by offering to lend them money to buy seeds and tools. The government also helps farmers to find buyers for their produce, for example selling pomegranates to Iran.

Food

The staple food of Afghanistan is wheat, which people use to make various kinds of bread. Rice is also very popular. It is used to make the national dish of spiced rice, called pullao. Most of the wheat is imported. This means that Afghans are badly affected when wheat prices rise. Most Afghans do not eat much meat. Instead they include plenty of vegetables, such as potatoes and spinach, and lots of yogurt in their diet. Across the country, one-third of Afghans do not eat enough healthy food to lead full and active lives. In some areas, charities give children free school meals and food to take home.

In drier regions of Afghanistan, where fertile land is rare, rearing sheep is one of the most widespread types of farming.

Transportation and Communications

In the countryside, most people travel and carry goods on foot or in carts pulled by horses and donkeys. In cities, people use taxis, buses, trucks, and rickshaws. There are only about half a million private cars in Afghanistan.

Roads

Afghanistan's road system is one of the worst in the world. Some of the roads that were destroyed during the Soviet occupation and wars have been rebuilt. However, roads can be dangerous because few drivers have passed tests and vehicles are often in poor condition or overloaded. The steep road from Kabul to Jalalabad that runs along the edge of deep gorges is thought to be the most dangerous in the world.

Facts at a Glance

Total Roads: 26,191 miles (42,150 km)

Paved Roads: 7,674 miles (12,350 km)

Major Airports: 7

▼ Afghanistan's rough, narrow mountain roads have few safety barriers, so drivers are at risk from accidents and from falling rocks.

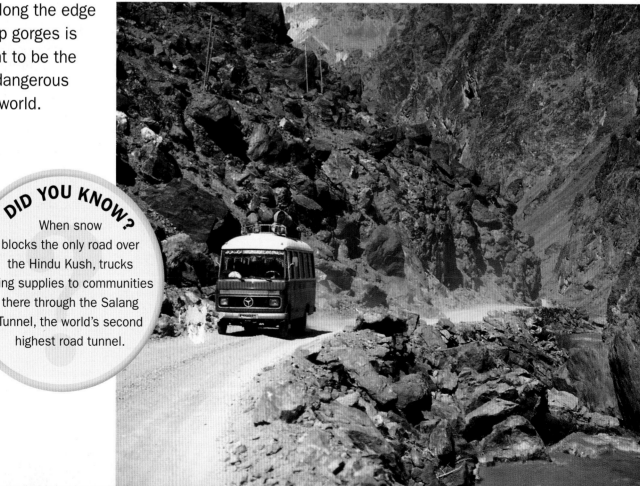

DID YOU KNOW?
When snow blocks the only road over the Hindu Kush, trucks bring supplies to communities there through the Salang Tunnel, the world's second highest road tunnel.

Rail, Air, and Sea

Afghan rulers in the past refused to build railways for fear that they would be used by foreign invaders. However, in 2010, the first railway line in Afghanistan was completed between Mazar-e-Sharif and Uzbekistan. Although airports were destroyed by wars, there are now 42 airports of different sizes and a national airline, called Ariana. Afghanistan is landlocked, but Afghan ships transport goods in and out of the Arabian Sea port of Chabahar, Iran.

Communication

The first cell phones in Afghanistan went on sale in 2001. By 2006, there were more than 3 million users. Today around 600,000 people use the Internet, mostly in Internet cafes or in schools. Using the Internet has made many people more aware of life in other countries and cultures. This is making some people question traditional Afghan customs, such as whether men and women should be allowed to meet openly in public.

▶ In 2001, the price of placing a call from a cell phone in Afghanistan was $2 a minute. However, it now costs 10 cents a minute to call and even less to send a text message.

▼ These Afghan men are being trained to use computers in a Jalalabad school. Computer education for children and adults can provide both job skills and access to global information.

Afghanistan: Internet and Cell Phone Use, 1995–2008

Millions

Cell phones in use

Internet subscribers

8
7
6
5
4
3
2
1
0

1995   2000   2005   2008

Years

Leisure and Tourism

During the Taliban years, many leisure activities were stopped. For example, it was against the law for people to fly kites. Women were banned from sports facilities. Today, such bans have been lifted and women take part in many activities and sports, including martial arts.

Leisure

Afghanistan's national sport is buzkashi, which is played mostly in northern Afghanistan. In buzkashi, teams of men on horseback try to lift a headless calf and put it into a scoring area. Afghans also enjoy soccer and a type of wrestling called ghosai.

▼ Buzkashi matches are rough and can last for days. They usually happen at special events, including carnivals, at which wrestling matches also take place.

Today, kite-makers are back in business and the skies are once more filled with colorful kite battles. Kite-flying is a game in which people try to cut opponents' kite strings using their own, which are often coated with ground glass and flour glue. Many Afghans also enjoy live music, going to the theater, attending poetry readings, watching television, and going to the movies.

Tourism

For most Afghans, a vacation means visiting relatives within the country. Few people can afford to travel abroad. Today not many tourists from abroad visit Afghanistan either. This is because of the threat posed by the fighting between NATO forces and the Taliban, and because there is not yet a tourist industry. However, there are tourist attractions, such as the great blue mosque in the ancient city of Mazar-e-Sharif and the dramatic mountain scenery.

In future, the country hopes to attract tourists to bring in money and development. In the 1960s and 1970s Afghanistan was a popular spot for mountain climbers. Today, some mountaineering companies are starting trips in the high northern mountain areas where there are unclimbed peaks and good weather for climbing.

▶ Climbing expeditions, such as this one in the Pamirs, bring in tourist income for Afghan locals, including guides and hotel owners.

Environment and Wildlife

Afghanistan is a wild and beautiful country. Within its forests and mountains there is a wide variety of wildlife. However, Afghanistan faces a major challenge in protecting its land and its animals from the threats posed by human activities.

Deforestation

Afghanistan faces several environmental issues. One is deforestation. Today, only 1 percent of the forests that originally covered the land remain. Although President Karzai banned logging in 2006, illegal logging is still a problem, especially in eastern Afghanistan. People cut trees to use the wood for building, heating, and cooking. Forests have also been affected by the long periods of drought.

Facts at a Glance

Proportion of Area Protected: 0.3%
Biodiversity (Known Species): 4,531

▼ The Band-e-Amir National Park was created in 2009 to help protect the wildlife of the region around the Band-e-Amir lakes.

Soil Degradation

Another environmental problem is soil degradation. The hot, dry climate causes soil erosion, which is when the fertile layer of topsoil is worn away. This has been made worse by overgrazing and deforestation. In some areas, the loss of topsoil has been so bad that the land has turned into desert. This has affected livestock and damaged wildlife populations.

Wildlife

Long-horned Marco Polo sheep, golden eagles, and mountain salamanders can be found in Afghanistan's mountains. In the deserts, there are goitered gazelles, porcupines, and camel spiders. The country is also home to nine different types of wild cat, from snow leopards and lynx to jungle cats. This varied wildlife is threatened by habitat destruction and hunting.

There are about 70 species in Afghanistan that are protected by law. In 2009, the country created its first national park. Band-e-Amir is an area of deep blue lakes in the Hindu Kush Mountains that is home to important wildlife species, such as the Afghan snow finch. The governments of Afghanistan, China, Pakistan, and Tajikistan are planning an international peace park to protect part of the Pamir Mountains, which link the four countries.

> **DID YOU KNOW?**
> Afghanistan is home to one of the world's least-known birds. The large-billed reed warbler was discovered in 1867 but not seen again until 2006. Today, these warblers are breeding.

⭘ The borders between Afghanistan, Pakistan, and China meet in the Pamirs. Snow leopards range across these mountains, so shared protection from hunters should mean their numbers will increase.

Glossary

amputation (am-pyuh-TAY-shun) Cutting off or removing.

climate (KLY-mut) The kind of weather a certain place has.

custom (KUS-tum) A practice common to many people in a place or a social class.

deforestation (dee-for-uh-STAY-shun) When most of the trees in a forest are cut down.

democratic (deh-muh-KRA-tik) Having to do with a government that is run by the people who live under it.

drought (DROWT) A period of dryness that hurts crops.

ethnic (ETH-nik) Relating to a group of people who have the same race, nationality, beliefs, and ways of living.

export (ek-SPORT) To send something to another place to be sold.

fertile (FER-tul) Good for making and growing things.

fertilizer (FUR-tuh-lyz-er) Something put in soil to help crops grow.

food aid (FOOD AYD) Food sent to feed people in countries where it is needed.

fossil fuel (FO-sul FYOOL) A fuel, such as coal, natural gas, or gasoline, that was made from plants that died millions of years ago.

habitat (HA-buh-tat) The kind of land where an animal or a plant naturally lives.

heat stroke (HEET STROHK) An illness due to overheating of the body that includes the inability to sweat and a dangerously high body temperature.

import (IM-port) A good brought from one country to another.

invade (in-VAYD) To enter a place to take it over.

irrigation (ih-rih-GAY-shun) The carrying of water to land through ditches or pipes.

Koran (KOR-ahn) The Islamic holy book.

land mine (LAND MYN) A bomb buried under ground to prevent people from crossing over certain areas of land.

madrassa (muh-DRAH-sah) Islamic school.

monsoon (mon-SOON) Period of heavy rain.

mortality rate (mor-TA-luh-tee RAYT) The percentage of people in an area who die over a certain period.

mosque (MOSK) A place of worship and prayer for Muslims.

national park (NASH-nul PARK) Land that is set aside by a country's government for people to visit and animals to live on.

natural resources (NA-chuh-rul REE-sors-ez) Things in nature that can be used by people.

occupied (AH-kyuh-pyd) Under the control of people from another country.

overgrazing (oh-ver-GRAYZ-ing) When animals eat too many of the plants in an area.

persecute (PER-sih-kyoot) To attack someone because of his or her beliefs.

polluted (puh-LOO-ted) Poisoned with certain kinds of bad matter.

refugee (reh-fyoo-JEE) A person who leaves his or her own country to find safety.

staple food (STAY-pul FOOD) A very important and basic food item.

terrorist (TER-er-ist) A person or a group that seeks to scare or threaten with violence illegally.

turban (TUR-bun) A long cloth that is wound around the head, worn mostly in Arabic Muslim countries.

Topic Web

Use this topic web to explore Afghan themes
in different areas of study.

Art
Many kites in Afghanistan are made from multi-colored paper with bold patterns or symbols. Design a kite of your own with an Afghan theme. For example, you could incorporate the colors of the Afghan flag in your design.

Science
Dirty water is the cause of many infectious diseases in Afghanistan. Find out more about how infectious diseases are transmitted through water. Draw a diagram to show the cycle of bacteria in water passing infectious diseases to people and how bacteria return to the water.

Math
The unit of currency in Afghanistan is the afghani, which is divided into 100 puls. In July 2010, $1 was the equivalent of 46 afghanis. Most people in Afghanistan live on $14 a week. Work out what this would be in afghanis.

History
Find out what you can about the Taliban's years of rule in Afghanistan. List the ways that they wanted Afghan people to behave and some of the laws they introduced.

Afghanistan

Geography
Find out more about how the geography of Afghanistan affects the lives of the people living there and how it is a factor in keeping the country poor.

Information Technology
Use the Internet to research some important people in recent Afghan history, such as Hamid Karzai, Mullah Mohammad Omar, and Osama bin Laden. How did they shape the current political situation?

Citizenship
Afghanistan is a very poor country. Draw a spider diagram to show how richer countries could help and the different types of aid Afghanistan needs. Think about things such as roads and buildings, water and electricity supplies, health, farmers, business people, families, and refugees.

English
Imagine you are a girl growing up in Afghanistan today. Write a letter to the Taliban explaining why you have a right to an education and to continue going to school with boys.

Further Reading, Web Sites, and Index

Further Reading

Afghanistan by Jovanka JoAnn Milivojevic (Heinemann-Raintree, 2011)
Afghanistan by Lisa Owings (Bellwether Media, 2011)
Focus on Afghanistan by Nikki Van Der Gaag (World Almanac Library, 2007)

Web Sites

Due to the changing nature of Internet links, PowerKids Press has developed an online list of Web sites related to the subject of this book. This site is updated regularly. Please use this link to access the list:
www.powerkidslinks.com/discovc/afghan/

Index